CW00983003

When Coal Was King In Fife

Andrew Farmer

© 2004 Andrew Farmer.
50, Norman Drive, Old Catton, Norwich, NR6 7HN

All Rights Reserved

ISBN 09527254-3-6

First published 2004

All rights reserved. No part of this book may be reproduced or transmitted in any form or by any means, electronically or mechanically, including photocopying, fax, recording, or any information storage or retrieval system with out prior permission from the copyright holder.

By the Same Author

Kinglassie, Mine Roots. 1995.   ISBN 0 9527254 0 1
Lamping the Flame.   1997.   ISBN 0 9527254 1 X
Coalfields, Callisthenics, Classrooms et al.
                       1995.   ISBN 1 900824 01 9
Kinglassie Village, A Mining Pedigree.
                       2000.   ISBN 0 9527254 2 8

Front cover
Miners at Bowhill Colliery.
From left to right:
Alex Smith, Tom Mair, David Ritchie, George McIvor.

Dedication

This book is unreservedly dedicated to my uncle, Alexander Mathieson, 1916 – 2003.

Very intelligent and widely-read himself, my uncle – whom I simply called 'Sandy' – helped and supported me through all of the critical learning and growing periods of my life. My poem, specially written for him a few years before he passed away, tries to say it all. That poem, entitled 'Smart Aleck', fittingly, is the first one in this book.

Sandy was, like so many of his generation, a miner through inheritance. He worked, from leaving school in 1930, at Bowhill Colliery (Fife) until its closure in 1965, a total of 35 years. His father, my maternal grandfather, John Mathieson, 1880-1941, had also worked there, and at nearby Dundonald Colliery, for over 40 years.

Sandy liked my mining poems, and it was his idea that I bring them all together in one volume. This I have now been able to do.

Andrew Farmer

The author, Andrew Farmer, (left) with
Sandy Mathieson, his uncle, in 2001

About The Author

1939 Born 5 July, survivor of premature twin boys of Alex and Jane Farmer (m/s Mathieson)

1940-45 Miner father enlisted in RAF, Andrew moves, with mother, from Kinglassie to Dundonald, to live with maternal grandparents. Formal school begins in Feb 1944, at Denend Primary.

1945-50 Father demobbed post-war, family returns to Kinglassie. Father resumes mining at local colliery, Andrew continues schooling at Kinglassie Primary.

1950-57 Began secondary education at Beath High School, in Cowdenbeath, a town with an industry, and a history, steeped in coal. In 1955 and 1956, Andrew is the top science student in his year group.

1957-61 Studied Chemistry, and allied subjects, at Edinburgh University for four years. In 1960, on an 8 week vacation job at the National Chemical Laboratory (Teddington), Andrew co-published a research paper in the Journal of Chomatography. In June 1961, he graduated with an honours degree in Chemistry, incorporating an inter-honours qualification in Mathematics. Andrew decided upon a career as a Science Teacher.

1961-62 Completes teacher training year at Moray House, Edinburgh. Completes studies for Diploma of Education (Dip. Ed) at Edinburgh University. Accepts science teaching post at Templehall Secondary School, in Kirkcaldy, Fife.

1962 Married Freda Smith on 3 August, in Edinburgh. Began teaching, in Kirkcaldy, on August 20.

1963 Moved from Edinburgh to Kirkcaldy to live.

1964 Daughter, Jacqueline, born on 6 Feb. She has Down's Syndrome. Teacher probationary period (2 years) successfully completed.

1965 Appointed Head of Chemistry in School, in July. Son, Peter, born on 17 Sept.

1966-67	Won major prize in the annual national competition "Guinness Awards for Science Teachers", for innovations in chemistry teaching. Met writer C P Snow, of "The Two Cultures" fame, at the London presentation ceremony. An inspirational contact for Andrew.
1969	Accepted "Head of Science" post at Earlham School, Norwich.
1970	Family moves south to Norwich in March. Andrew takes up new post in April.
1971	Family moves into Old Catton, a suburb of Norwich, in April.
1972	Son, Richard, born in August, date coincides with Andrew and Freda's 10th wedding anniversary.
1974-77	Research study at University of East Anglia (UEA), on part-time basis. Awarded Master of Philosophy degree (M.Phil) in June, 1977.
1978-82	Further research studies, at UEA, again on a part-time basis within the School of Chemical Education. Awarded degree of Doctor of Philosophy (Ph.D) in June, 1982.
1982-85	Father dies on 31/12/81. Andrew begins to research into, and to write about his family roots and mining background. Prose gradually phases into narrative verse. Produces a manuscript of poems, "Shadows in the Dark", for circulation within family and close friends. Son, Peter, seriously injured, and disabled, in car accident in June 1984. To help Freda cope, Andrew relinquishes some school responsibilities.
1989	An eye examination, for new spectacles, detects chronic glaucoma in both eyes. One eye operated upon in June. In August, whilst holidaying in Amsterdam, Andrew and Freda are both seriously injured in a street accident with a car. A drink-driving incident is subsequently confirmed. The operation on Andrew's second eye, further damaged in the accident, is delayed until Nov.
1990	Andrew retires from teaching, on medical grounds, after 20 years at Earlham School.

1991-94	Through 'creative writing' courses at a local Adult Education College, Andrew begins to write with publication in mind. An early poem, "Bird's-Eye View", originally part of his 'Shadows in the Dark' manuscript (1985), had already been published in 1990, as the introduction to the booklet, 'Kinglassie – A Village Remembered', produced by a WEA Local History group.
1995	Published first book, 'Kinglassie – Mine Roots'
1997	Published second book, 'Lamping the Flame'
1998	Andrew is awarded first prize in an annual 'Poet of the Year' competition organised by the Norfolk-based publishing company Hilton House. His winning entry was a selection of 10 mining poems. First grandchild, Cai, a son for Richard and partner, is born in Dec.
1999	Hilton House publish a new selection of Andrew's poems. The booklet, entitled "Coalfields, Callisthenics, Classrooms et al' is dedicated to grandson Cai.
2000	Published third book, 'Kinglassie Village: A Mining Pedigree', also dedicated to Cai.
2002	Son, Richard, father of Cai, dies in a car crash, in May.
2003	Andrew produces a commemorative biography about Richard – for family, close friends, and, ultimately for Cai himself when he matures. Restricted circulation. Last remaining relative, Uncle Sandy (Mathieson) passes away in July, aged 87 years. This book is dedicated to him.

Foreword

Andrew Farmer, or Drew as he was known, and I grew up in the small mining village of Kinglassie in Fife where both our fathers were miners. Drew was seven months my senior and in a class ahead of me at Primary School. However the community was such that all the scholars knew one another to a greater or lesser degree as did our parents. The pit and mine were predominant in our young lives; we were familiar with mining jargon and we knew the difference between firedamp and blackdamp. The words "roof fall" which flashed occasionally through the village sent an icy hand into the gut; had someone been injured or perhaps killed? However the years passed, Drew went off to University, and I started work, and like many others we lost touch.

We were probably the first generation of miners sons to move away from the industry. I was aware early on that I did not possess the necessary attributes to follow my father down the pit. I left school in 1955 and started work as an apprentice Television Engineer, the following seven years were spent repairing them. In 1963 I decided to expand my horizons and I joined the Ministry of Aviation who ran the UKs Air Traffic Control Service. In 1972 the service transferred to the newly formed Civil Aviation Authority and I retired as Head of Communications Engineering at the Scottish and Oceanic Air Traffic Control Centre at Prestwick, having been eternally grateful to my Science Master who had introduced me into the world of electronics.

Fate has some strange ways of working. Around the beginning of 1999 I was browsing the internet and I came across a book of poetry entitled "Kinglassie - Mine Roots" written by an Andrew Farmer. I had to wonder - was this the Drew Farmer that I had known so many years ago? Via a circuitous route through his publisher I made contact by telephone. Names and faces long forgotten suddenly came to life and the years fell away - we were back home as boys in Kinglassie. We have maintained contact since that day and I have been privileged to receive copies of all Drew's publications. His mining poems are extremely evocative, but they bring to me a degree of sadness not just of the passing years but by encapsulating the human elements of mining and bringing to life the memories of the daily backbreaking toil under constant life threatening conditions in which our fathers worked. I am aware there are those who mourn the passing of the mining industry and a way of life that was familiar to so many in this country. However I am sure there are many sons and grandsons who are grateful that they can feel the heat of the sun, the rain on their faces and breathe clean fresh air, something that was denied to their fathers and grandfathers for a third of their working lives.

In this book Drew has captured the essence of the mining industry and the conflicts which occurred in the 1920s. It gives a vivid insight into the social struggles to improve working conditions in the face of fierce opposition from the mine owners and indeed the government at the time. Our generation are beholden to these men who fought and faced imprisonment in their efforts to advance the industry in which our fathers spent their working lives.

Unlike Drew my mining heritage is a mere 40 years. My father Frank, along with two pals, left the North-East town of Montrose and came to Kinglassie to find work in the pit. It must have seemed to these young men a strange and hostile environment; nevertheless there they remained, working until retirement and living in the village until their deaths. Although mining has touched just one generation of my family it has undoubtedly left it's mark on me; I will always be a Miner's Son.

I am pleased to have been able to make a small contribution to Drew's research for this worthy volume.

Francis Allan Ferrier
Doonfoot Ayr
June 2004

Contents

Photographic Material and other Illustrations

Acknowledgement and thanks for providing, and for giving permission to use where appropriate, some of the photos herein is made to the following individuals or sources:

Photo, front cover, miners at Bowhill Colliery – Mr Dan Imrie, ex-miner, of Kinglassie

Map, rear cover, coalfields of Fife – from "The Mining Kingdom" (Guthrie Hutton, 1999)

Photo page 11, author and Uncle Sandy – Freda Farmer, wife of author

Photo page 35, three lads on pithead, 1926 – author's mother (deceased)

Photo page 41, Kinglassie Colliery – Record Book of Veteran Employees (Fife Coal Co. 1945)

Photo page 43, Valleyfield Disaster, 1939 – A History of the Scottish Miners (R Page Arnot, 1955)

Photo page 53, miner Adam Currie at coalface, Bowhill – Mr Dan Imrie, ex-miner, of Kinglassie

Page 59, 'Foreword' – Record Book of Veteran Employees (Fife Coal Co. 1945)

Page 62, Andrew Farmer, the author's grandfather. Veteran Miners – Record Book of Veteran Employees (Fife Coal Co. 1945)

Page 65, Alexander Blair. Veteran Miners – Record Book of Veteran Employees (Fife Coal Co. 1945)

Photo page 69, Coal Queen entrants, Kinglassie – Mr Alex Brewster, ex-miner, of Dundee.

Page 78, Thomas Erskine. Veteran Miners – Record Book of Veteran Employees (Fife Coal Co. 1945)

Photo page 85, Author and grandson – Freda Farmer, wife of the author.

Text References

1.   The Rise of the Parish Coal Industry, Vols 1 and 2.

2.   Acts of the Parliaments of Scotland, Vol IV.

3.   Hamilton, MSS, 592 (2), bdls 4-8.

4.   A History of the Scottish Miners – R. Page Arnot (1955)

5.   Bowhill Colliery Mining Disaster – Dan Imrie/Alan Watkins. (A Commemorative Booklet, published 31 October, 2001).

6.   The Recollections of John McArthur from 'Militant Miners'.

7.   Service: Record Book of Veteran Employees in the Services of the Fife Coal Company Limited August, 1945.

8.   Fife; The Mining Kingdom, - Guthrie Hutton (1999)

The above reference sources, labelled 1-8, have been used within prose sections of this book where indicated.

Smart Aleck

By choice, he'd always preferred
Nightshift at the local mine,
Leaving to toil deep down below
Just when the rest of us
Were making preparations for bed

Then he'd get back when dawn
Was breaking, flecks of coal dust
Still upon eyelids and ears only
Part washed, tired, yet in dire need
Of a rejuvenating mug of tea.

Which he'd brewed himself, slurping it
Noisily, with measured pleasure, before
Then paying heed to the needs
Of the two incumbents, slowly stirring,
Sharing the living-room bed settee

That was my grandmother and me,
A boy aged three, but aspiring
To be four, awakened, and suddenly
Desperate to be led bathroom-wise
For a urgent usually misdirected pee.

Whilst my widowed gran, still abed,
Tucked into the fresh-brewed tea
And toasted bread, becoming much more
Ready to face her own day
Of busy domesticity and family chores.

Which included looking after me,
For my mother, fast asleep elsewhere,
Would rise to a factory job
A long bus ride away, doing her
Share of keeping Hitler at bay.

For my dad, who'd years before
Leapt at the chance to take arms
Against that rampaging foe, was now
Middle East based, facing hot sun
And sand, maintaining Monty's desert advance.

Thus leaving Uncle Sandy, erstwhile
Brewer of morning tea, and hewer
Of coal that kept the home fires
And factory furnaces burning bright,
As main man in my life.

Not only during the blackout years
Of that longer than expected war,
But afterwards too, for when
My father returned, sunburnt and safe,
He seemed like a stranger to me.

Sadly, Dad had simply been away
Too long, missing my early critical
Pre-school childhood years, and then
Some more, a gap in shared
Experience too significant to ignore.

For it was Sandy who'd tried,
Too late, to break my fall
From an icy level crossing gate,
Before carrying me home again, my arm
Fractured, my mind numb with pain.

And it was he who'd been
The butt of my boyhood pranks,
Taking cheeky remarks, piggy-back rides,
Impish interruptions to his daytime
Naps, very much in his stride.

Then, later, that erudite self-educated
Mining man had shaped my own scholastic
Grasp of musical notation, dreaded algebraic
Equation, and interpretation of bards, Burns
And Shakespeare, whenever it became necessary.

And so, without Uncle Sandy being
There, to encourage, sustain, and nurture
The only child that was me, then
To be sure, I wouldn't have become
The man I'm now fortunate to be.

Forget-We-Not

Old friend, let's just wallow
In nostalgia, and appreciate
At long last, the contours
Of our lives, shaped by experiences
Now imbued with a significance
We'd not previously discerned.

For Old Age does indeed have
Fruits to savour, a rich blend
Of reflections upon and insights
Into the frailties of the human
Condition, that only now begin
To make sense in our maturity.

Together, we can share memories,
And shed a tear for friends
Departed, for other lives touched,
For opportunities missed because of how
Things once were, letting our reminiscences
Illuminate some forgotten corners of Yesteryear.

A Child Listening

Sometimes, noises he made, coughing
Deep down in his chest, or moving around
In a bed whose springs, creaking,
Had known better days, were sounds
Which drifted through the night curtain
Strung across the recess that isolated me
From them, and which made certain
That what I heard I couldn't see.

Of course he tried to be quiet
When he rose, well before dawn
Had decided to push the night
Away, but each sound, even a yawn,
Seemed to be magnified, in a blackness
Softened only by the rather eerie
Glow of a mantle, having little success
In trying to keep darkness at bay.

The now familiar noises that crept
Through into my curtained recess,
Like the winding of the watch that kept
Good time, helped me follow the progress
Of his preparations, the unaltered routine
To be gone through, before he might
Feel ready to leave for the mine,
And quietly slip out into the night.

But just before be clicked the latch
Of the door, there were low whisperings,
In words that I couldn't quite catch,
Then the soft sound of lips kissing,
And he was gone. Soon the stillness
Crept back, the mantle ceased to burn,
And I closed my eyes as darkness
Descended, willing sleep to return.

Early Days

"The collieries in Fife had been the most important and numerous in Scotland in the seventeenth century"
(Ref 1)

"In 1606, Scottish mine owners succeeded in getting the Scottish Parliament to pass a statute which declared that neither hewers nor bearers could be employed by a new master without a testimony from their old master, or an attestation from a magistrate"
(Ref 2)

"If any hewer or bearer left their employment without permission they were to be reckoned as thieves, and punished accordingly"
(Ref 2)

"In testimony, given in 1720, in connection with the Duke of Hamilton's colliery at Kinglassie, we learn that the father of the family usually worked as a hewer, and that his wife acted as his bearer, and tried to prevent the grieve from short-measuring her husband who was paid on a piece-work basis of between 7s and 8s per week"
(Ref 3)

"Cases of women serving as hewers can be found. In 1727, at Kinglassie, three of the twenty-four hewers were women"
(Ref 3)

Lamping The Flame

Hugging the roof spaces,
Hovering unseen,
Lurked hellfire itself,
Predating the cloven face
For incautious Man,
And his dancing naked flame.

For no light of day
Could breach that total dark,
Scores of fathom below,
To show just where
Virgin coal seams lay,
Waiting to be stripped bare.

And so such nakedness
Had to be sheathed,
To screen out heat from light,
And by inhibiting full consumation
Between firedamp and flame,
Helped save lives.

Putting Away Childish Things

I sampled the taste of Hell
On my first day below,
Working alongside my dad
Deep inside that claustrophobic hole.

In the inky blackness, lamp flames
Flickered within their discrete
Globes of light, distorting shadows,
And etching faces with strain.

Sickening smells, tallow tinged with
Carbide vapours produced by those
Inadequate lamps, wafting upon
Dust-filled air, assailed my lungs.

His bare torso dirt-caked
And streaked with sweat,
Dad cut deep with his mighty pick,
Cleaving coal clean from seam.

Unused to such hard shovelling
In confined space, my young limbs
Soon cramped with the effort
Of trying to match his fierce pace.

Only piece-time offered any relief
From toil, and the chance to excrete
Discreetly into waste, and to meet
And eat at a makeshift howff.

Afterwards, as we trudged home,
Coal-blackened, hungry, and tired,
Our shift done, I suddenly realised
That childhood too was behind me.

A Proud Pedigree

Impoverished in all but spirit,
Work-hardened, their expectation
That life together, for them,
Would be infinitely preferable
To simply remaining apart,
Was realised, without affectation,
When my great-grandparents married
In 1885, at Kinglassie Parish Church.

A union durable enough to withstand
The agonies of unemployment pain,
And a Great War that claimed
Their staunchly patriotic eldest lad,
Whilst, closer to home,
There were the inevitable self-sacrifices
Needed to sustain the well-being
Of the nine lives that remained.

Youngsters destined to become either
Domestics, farmhands, or brash colliers,
A harsh inheritance
Softened only by long awaited reforms
In education, housing, and health,
Designed to remove forever
The inequities of social deprivation,
A legacy for my generation,
And for those that succeeded us,
Worth much more than mere wealth.

A Fiery Passion

Life interred, its beauty deferred,
Is reformed, inside, into facets
Of immense power. A deformation
Denied space, assets in strength,
Trapped in a length of coalface.

Age and potency, incompatibles entwined,
Yet unconfined, once the hot breath
Of sweet fresh air begins to flow,
Releasing instantly, all that took aeons
To store, as ore, deep down below.

And what appears to be desecration,
The death throes of coal exhumed,
Is, in truth, a dance full of passion,
A frenetic celebration of liberation,
Proclaimed in flame, and colour, and form.

For therein lies near immortality,
Though ash into ashes it may be,
As leaves, long nurtured by light,
And kissed by midday sun, survive
In coal, an essence of soul lives on.

The Fife Coal Company

Background

The Fife Coal Company was formed in 1872, initially to take over and develop the pits belonging to the Beath and Blairadam Coal Company. The first Chairman of the company was William Lindsay, then the Provost of Leith. In 1875, Charles Carlow, the first manager of the company, married Mary Lindsay, daughter of the Director, and the couple settled in Kelty. Their son, Charles Augustus Carlow (C A Carlow), entered service with the Fife Coal Company in 1896.

After qualifying as a colliery manager, he assisted his father – who became Chairman after the death of William Lindsay – in the capacity of manager, Joint Managing Director (appointed 1923), and subsequently as Chairman from 1939. His involvement in the pits was total. Anecdotally, he writes thus:

"My chief recollection regarding Lumphinans No. XI Pit is in connection with the outburst of carbon monoxide in 1906, resulting in the death of two miners – Alex Black and Tom Serrie. I led the rescue party in an effort to save these men's lives. The only protection we had was the canary which I took out of the kitchen before starting for the pit. Everybody seemed surprised, but I carried the canary and the men followed me. To our regret we were unsuccessful. It may be that some of the "Old Timers" referred to in this book of service were in the rescue party, and may remember stepping over the bodies of horses overcome by the gas, and our sense of frustration when the canary kept falling off its perch and we had to go back". (Ref 7)

The period from 1880 onwards saw many takeovers of existing coal companies, and the sinking of many new pits that formed the basis of the coal industry in Fife. The list is an impressive litany of growth, viz. Lindsay Pit (1876), Wellsgreen Pit (1884), Cowdenbeath No. 10 (1887), Aitken Pit (1893), Bowhill (1895), Lumphinans No. XI (1896), Mary Pit (1902), Kinnaird (1904), Kinglassie (1908). The list is not exhaustive, but is an accurate reflection of the demands for good Fife coal pre- First World War.

Two wars later, and decades of substantial miner unrest in between, by 1945 the Fife Coal Company was the largest coal producer in Scotland. But, politically, the days of the private coal owner were numbered. On 1 Jan, 1947, known as 'Vesting Day', the mines were nationalised and the National Coal Board (NCB) came into existence.

Fife continued to see major pit developments, namely at Rothes and Seafield, the establishment of huge power stations at Kincardine and Longannet (vast appetites for coal), but, because of the growing popularity of other fuel sources viz. nuclear, oil, and gas, the overall market for coal was shrinking. The 1960's saw the closure of many deep mines across central Fife, a process which continued piece-meal throughout the 1970's and 1980's.

The last great national strike of 1984 signalled the death-knell of not only the coal industry in Britain, but also of a substantial diminution of union authority within it and other associated industries. Politically, King Coal was unceremoniously dethroned. Mining villages, and the community spirit endemic within such a close-knit society, simply died out across the coal producing areas of Britain. An era of greatness was over. (Refs 7 and 8)

A Company Concession

The passage to ground was rough, and accompanied
By a rumble loud enough to disturb many doors down,
As huge unfettered lumps, competing to be first out
Of the tipper lorry, crashed hard onto cobblestone,
Raising a cloud of black dust that hung around
In the air long after the sound itself had gone.

Time enough for faces to appear at various windows
Along the street, drawn by the need to know
Which house had just been delivered of some coal,
Free of course to miners, a perk of their most
Demanding of trades, now forming an obstruction
On the front path awaiting the shovel of mine host.

For that half-ton load had to be moved, a barrowful
At a time, trundled from its brief squat by the gate
To wherever the bunker or coalhouse happened to be,
Leaving behind it on the pavement tell tale signs
Of what had recently lain there, an ingrained imprint
That would remain until the rain could wash it free.

Great Expectations

Grey skies, a cold dawn creeping
Out of the remnants of night,
Red-slated houses, occupants sleeping,
Painted by pale shafts of light.

Drab streets, deserted and windswept,
Cobbles polished, wet enough to glisten.
Silent; then the sound of footsteps
As someone braves the drizzling rain.

A man, cloth-capped, long of stride,
Head lowered to shield his face,
With two dogs trotting side by side,
A trio out walking at running pace.

Greyhounds, rubbing haunch and shoulder,
Racers, sharing a leash of chain and leather,
One, just a pup, the other much older,
Panting heavily, taking exercise together.

Lean of shank, protruding rib cage,
Lolling pink tongues seeking cool air,
Bound in harness, Youth and Old Age,
Making rather an ill-matched pair.

Their footsteps pass, then fade away,
From the houses no sound at all,
Night has flown, it is a new day,
And the rain continues to fall.

Brief Encounter

Her half of the bed did not feel warm
To my touch, the rumpled sheets the only
Evidence that she'd lain there at all.

Through habit, she always rose very early,
Meeting each new day just as the dawn
Broke to sweep the darkness away.

Her sounds, a poker clinking in the grate,
A shovel scraping ash across the hearth,
Seemed too harsh for the prevailing calm.

Yet, a new fire had to be kindled,
Its crackling coal giving birth to flames
That flickered and danced in the chimney.

And water, at rest in the flue tank,
Spurred into action by these tongues
Of heat, soon sizzled with latent energy.

For only then could she begin to boil
The stench of sweat and grime out of the clothes
I'd soiled during a nightshift at the mine.

And at last, I was able to have a wash,
Crouched, chin on knees, in a tin tub
Drawn up close to the warming blaze.

Taking pleasure in the too brief intimacy
Of touch, as she helped scrub clean
Parts of me I couldn't quite reach.

Gentle hands, yet strong enough to wring
My dripping clothes free of their wet,
Before pegging them out on the drying line.

Leaving me to crawl between cold sheets,
To snatch a few hours of daytime sleep,
Disappointed that she was no longer lying there.

Out to Grass

Crows chattering in the treetops
Overhead, a babble in the branches,
Contrasts starkly with his stillness,
A solitary figure cropping grass,
Munching ruminatively in his own
Little corner of a fenced meadow.

Unlike the cackling black carrion
Up above, he has longevity,
And a past that resides within him
Still, in his bowed over-taxed
Frame, his dust-matted mane,
And the damaged unseeing eyes.

Despite the freedom to graze
Unconfined, he moves around by touch,
And scent, nuzzling for a sweet clover
Amongst the host of wild flower,
For he sees little more than before,
Whilst working below, hauling hutches of ore.

Sharing stable space with scuttling mice,
Caged canaries, and flies that swarmed
In the lamplights of miners cutting coal
From face, harnessing equine power to move
It from there to elsewhere, a union
Of labours in an era long gone.

Troubled Days
The Great Lock-Out of 1921

Background

The miners never accepted 1921 as a strike; they always claimed that it was a lock-out. The Government had decontrolled the mines just beforehand, and the owners issued an ultimatum that the mines would only continue provided reductions in wages were accepted by the miners. In this way they also gave notice to the safety workers who were also employed in the pits. So for the first time in trade union history the miners and safety men took joint action. The labour of everyone who worked in the pits was withdrawn – tradesmen, safety workers, pump men, winding enginemen joined the miners who were locked out.

Meanwhile, in Fife, as elsewhere, the coal owners tried to keep the pumps going by recruiting scab labour. They were able to man a number of pits with misguided students, colliery officials and clerks.

Before very long, this, in almost every part of Fife, resulted in spontaneous mass meetings of the men objecting to the steam-raising and pumping at collieries being continued by blacklegs. The mass meetings decided to march on the respective pits and demand the withdrawal of this blackleg labour. (Ref 4)

The Action in Fife

"Abe Moffat and I went to Kinglassie one day and slept the night on the fireside rug in the single-end of the couple who put us up. We went down to the pit next morning.

Moffat had finished speaking, and I had started to speak when the police arrived. A rumpus started. A lad was aiming a punch at me, but Moffat stepped in and got his face smashed. But the miners stopped that from developing further.

We decided to go back to Kinglassie on the following Sunday, 3 April, in strength. We assembled the whole of our speaking team, brought together people from Bowhill, Lochgelly and surrounding districts, and, behind a pipe band, marched the three miles into Kinglassie. Almost everybody in the village turned out to our meeting, perhaps wondering whether it was going to be a donnybrook or not". (Ref 6)

"At Cowdenbeath, on Tues. April 5, the miners held a meeting at the Empire Theatre. Whilst they planned a march to Kirkford Pit (Cowdenbeath No.10), to demand that under-managers there – under the direction of one William Spalding, a general manager of the Fife Coal Company itself – stop acting as boiler-firemen, outside the theatre, the Pipe Band paraded the High Street. After the meeting was over, several thousand men, led by union officials, and headed by Cowdenbeath Pipe Band, noisily made their way to Kirkford Pit". (Ref 4)

"At Kirkford Pit, despite police presence, there were enough strikers to forcibly 'draw the fires' and put the pumps out of action. The men got hold of William Spalding himself, and frog-marched him back to the town centre. Police numbers there had swelled considerably, largely due to busloads of officers being drafted in from surrounding areas. The police managed to effect a rescue of the now bedraggled Spalding, and hurriedly transported him from the scene in a hastily commandeered tramcar. An ugly situation then developed, in which police batons were wielded and stones were thrown in response. There were injuries on both sides. Only one man, a middle-aged miner, William Easton, was arrested. Later that evening, around 10pm, the police, now seventy strong, cleared the High Street of demonstrators in one massive baton charge. An eventful day was over".

"Next morning, Wed 6 April, William Easton was brought before the Sheriff at Dunfermline and charged with assaulting the police and other public order offences. He was transferred to Edinburgh prison to await his trial.

One week later, in the early hours of Wed. 13 April, the police swooped on houses in Cowdenbeath, Lumphinous and Lochgelly. Eight men were arrested as they slept. In due course, on 13 June, at the High Court in Perth, these eight, and William Easton, were duly tried for a series of public order and other offences. Easton, and two others, were sentenced to 12 months imprisonment. Three other men were given 6 months, and the remaining three simply admonished by the court". (Ref 4)

"On that self-same Wednesday morning, 13 April, the rate-payers of Cowdenbeath awoke to find that the burgh had, overnight, become converted into an army camp. Bus loads of soldiers and marines had poured into the town, and also into nearby Lochgelly. Even the more distant village of Kinglassie had acquired its own ring of armed steel. West Fife mining communities were now under military occupation for the rest of that summer. Mass meetings and marches were banned". (Ref 4)

"Week by week the struggle had dragged on. Government terms had been firmly rejected by the miners. Union ballots had revealed a 78% opposition to acceptance.
But families were beginning to feel the pinch of protracted unemployment. On July 1, 1921, the long drawn-out conflict was ended by a decision to return to work.
But for many work was scarce. Wages had been driven down below their pre-1914 level, and many pits remained idle.
By Oct. 1921, there were 22,000 former miners unemployed, and 45,000 only partially employed, across the Scottish coalfields. Fife bore its share of this unrelenting penury. It would take another three years before conditions, above and below ground, improved for mining families. But 1926 heralded yet another lock-out and its consequent lengthy struggle with the coal-owners. Industrial strife was fast becoming endemic in the life of the coalminer". (Ref 4).

Picket

Was yesterday just some dreadful dream,
Or was that nightmarish scene
Real, the fighting, the violence, a scream
That was mine, the terrible searing
Pain, a horse, frightened, rearing,
Bruising my back, rupturing my spleen.

Fear is no stranger to a mine,
Yet, cold shivers caress my spine
Recalling the menace of that broad blue line,
A wedge, a concentration of beef and brawn,
Acting out a role, just uniformed pawns
Dancing to a political tune.

Hospitalised, my body wracked with pain,
The hapless victim of industrial mayhem,
Emotions mixed, anger refusing to wane,
Cursing comrades who insist upon working,
Opening a wound, a rift that is hurting,
Close camaraderie is dying of shame.

Hole In The Family Tree

Who can say
What really happened
On that sun-kissed day
In mid-July.

For in less time
Than it takes to blink
An eye - a young miner
Suddenly began to die.

Conscious, and horrifyingly aware
Of the life fast-seeping
From a gaping gunshot tear
Deep inside his thigh,

The spreading crimson stain
On the roadside grass
Bringing grief - and pain,
And the endless questioning

Why it had to happen
So far away - from aid,
And from those who cared.
Perhaps - only God can say.

(Commemorates the tragic death of Andrew Farmer, age 19 years, on 21 July, 1921 - during the miners 'Great Lock-Out' of that year. Andrew, a miner himself - killed by the accidental discharge of a friend's shotgun - was 'the uncle' the author never met.)

First job on pithead after leaving school. Taken in 1926.
Left to right: Alex Farmer (author's father), Peter Moyes, Andrew
Mercer, all aged 14 years

Dust on the Crystal Ball

Sometimes, during the long summer holiday
From school, if the weather was fine,
I used to nip along, after the midday
Horn had blown, to the mouth of the mine,

Searching for a face I could always recognise,
Even amongst the look-alike crowd
Of miners, all wearing the same coal dust disguise,
Emerging from that hole in the ground.

On spotting me, he would wink an eye,
And teeth would flash, white framed in black.
Then two sinewed arms would hoist me high
To sit upon his broad muscled back,

For despite him having been down
Since dawn, and probably aching in every bone,
My dad was always pleased I'd come
To chum him on the long walk back home,

And to share a laugh in the warming sun,
As he pretended to buckle under the load
Of a fast-growing lad, who would all too soon
Become strong enough to cut coal, beside his dad.

Free As A Bird

That distant speck of sky,
Approaching fast, soon profiles
Against an infinity of blue,
As he hurtles on, homing
In true, coming for grain,
And his slice of racing fame.

One in a flock of many,
Released in some faraway place,
He's flown well, across terrain
Unknown, his sense of space
And computing brain, unerringly,
Navigating him safely back home.

To make eyes at the sun,
Or to commune with clouds
High above an undulating sea,
Yet still fly home for tea,
Is what being free truly means
To a miner, earthbound like me.

Bird's-eye View (of Kinglassie)

Between the Miners' Institute
And the old church hall, skirting the edge
Of a field kept grassed for cattle,
A track of flattened clover traces the route
To a local landmark, Blythe's Tower,
Erected on top of the highest hill
Overlooking the village.

From up there, like an artery
Feeding a vital organ, the main street threads
Between red-tiled houses and shops
Until it reaches the hump bridge, and then stops.
For there it meets the Lochty, a modest river
That severs the village from its cemetery
Beyond, and keeps the living apart from the dead.

Before obliquely changing direction to flow
Parallel to, but perhaps a quarter mile
Below, the main street. On its other bank
The shaft has been sunk, a railway laid, and rows
Of miners' cottages built, each abode no more
Than a room and kitchen, topped by grey tiles,
And much plagued by water rats and damp.

Viewed from the tower, against a patchwork of heath
And fields stitched together with dry-stone dykes,
The colliery, with its permanent grime, and chain
Of shunting coal wagons, stands out like
A jagged tear, a surface sore
Disfiguring almost flawless terrain,
With the hint of even worse underneath.

Note: This poem was used as the introduction, in 1990, to the booklet 'Kinglassie – A Village Remembered', published and produced by a WEA Local History Group.

The Pit Rows

Cosily reclining face to face,
Sandwiched between Lochty burn and pithead,
The twin rows almost embraced
Through front gardens, only an access
Road inhibiting greater intimacy.

Consequently, the snug closeness
Of those Coal Company abodes,
Built just beside the colliery itself,
Simply guaranteed that a community
Was delivered virtually ready-made.

Starved of mains electricity,
Domestic survival depended upon
Bowhill-piped gas, and water
Filched directly from deep within
Those underground workings next door.

A convenient aquatic redistribution
Between home and over-damp mine,
Ensuring that daily accretions
Of coal grime upon working clothes,
Could be tubbed and scrubbed away.

For each scullery played host
To a huge stone-clad boiler
Greedy for coal, which belched
Steam, and regurgitated enough heat
To steep soiled garments for hours.

Whilst nearby, an enormous hob grate,
Fuelled by free coal, kept wintry
Chills at bay, created golden toast
From fork-held bread, and gently
Allowed precious moleskins to fender dry,

As daily, cramped in a tin tub
Too small to sprawl into, nakedness
Sought warmth and a discreet wash
Beside the fire, an embarrassing
Necessity in houses denied a bathroom.

In that doubly-recessed kitchen,
And in the back bedroom beyond
The long lobby, was suspended the only
Illumination in house, as hissing mantles
Suffused the darkness with eerie gloom.

An eerieness that seemed to pervade
Even the narrow rutted rows after dusk,
With street lamps, spawning more shadow
Than light, conjuring up phantom-like shapes
That frightened all but the brave.

But by day, it was quite different,
As a concentration of youngsters
Played endless street games, with paldies,
Headers, hide-and-seek, and ageless
Leeve-oh, usually occupying centre stage,

Yet, they were careful not to disturb
Elders appraising quoits thrown high
And true, catching sun on their way down
To ground also used by strapping youths
Exuberantly kicking a laced football around.

All simple shared recreations that helped
Keep hope and community spirit
Alive in the rows, enabling family life there
To thrive during those memorable decades
When King Coal reigned supreme in Fife.

Kinglassie Colliery, adjoining Pit Rows, 1945

41

Shadows Of Nostalgia

It was early dark,
But we'd had our tea,
And a short play
Out in the cobbled rows,
Beneath colliery-powered lamps
That spawned more shadow
Than light enough to host
Another few final rounds
Of timeless 'Leeve-Oh'.

And then to bed,
Comforted by the soporific glow
Of crackling concessionary coal
Throwing mesmeric dancing shadows
Upon the wall, as embers
Expired to ash, with a sigh,
And a flourish of flickering flame.

All against a backdrop,
Enacted at ceiling height,
Of the almost inaudible hiss
From gas, turned down low,
Flaring inside its mantle,
And casting incandescence
Upon the fire dance below.

This poem, one of over 200 entries for the Fife Fringe Open Poetry
Competition of 1999, was specially selected for public display in
the Lochgelly Centre, and later published in the competition
anthology 'Answering the Call'.

Valleyfield Colliery Disaster, Fife, October 1939
Wives and children waiting for news

Tragic Days

"On 26 August, 1901, at Donibristle Colliery, near Cowdenbeath, an inrush of surface moss into the mine workings below led to the loss of 8 lives. Only the courage of rescuers prevented a greater tragedy.

Four men were smothered and suffocated by the initial inflow of moss. An oversman, Rattray, and three other men, persisted in a rescue attempt. Their bodies were never recovered.

Up above, on a track of land aptly named Moss Moran, a huge chasm, hundreds of yards in circumference, had formed. A large crowd soon gathered at the site, which, through weight of numbers on the unstable moss, posed an additional danger to men still trapped below.

Rescue was initiated from above. Three volunteers, using wire ropes, descended into the gaping chasm and brought out 5 men. Two rescuers, who went back in to search for a missing miner, were themselves trapped by a further in-rush of moss, thought to be caused by crowd pressure.

On 29 August, at 2am, a volunteer rescuer – a miner, Robert Low, from Cowdenbeath – was lowered carefully into the chasm to search for the trapped men. He succeeded – returning with the last survivor and the two entombed rescuers. Later, bodies of only 3 of the 8 victims were recovered.

Almost fifty years later, on 7 Sept, 1950, at Knockshinnoch Colliery, in Ayrshire, a similar, but much larger, in-rush of surface moss caused an even greater tragedy, and loss of lives". (Ref 4).

"On 31st October, 1931, at Bowhill Colliery (West Fife), 10 miners lost their lives in an underground gas explosion. Nine of the victims – including two brothers – were local village men, the tenth came from Kingskettle.

Had it not been a Saturday, with only a repair crew on duty, then many more lives would have been lost.

Ironically, only two months earlier, the village had mourned the tragic loss of another of its young – and nationally famous – miner sons. This was John Thomson, aged 21 years, goalkeeper supreme of Celtic and Scotland. Tragically, John died from head injuries sustained during a Glasgow derby match against their great rivals, Rangers. The date, also a Saturday, was 5th September, 1931.

Both funerals, the first in September, the latter, a collective one, in November, attracted a cortege huge enough to swamp the village streets". (Ref 5)

"On 28 October, 1939, at Valleyfield Colliery on the Fife side of the River Forth, 35 miners lost their lives in an underground gas explosion.

At a subsequent inquiry, the mine owners, the Fife Coal Company, and some of their colliery management team, were fined for breach of Safety Regulations, specifically for those relating to the storage of explosives and to their safe use underground.

Up above, on the River Forth itself, on that self-same day of 28 October, 1939, the first raid upon the UK took place. German planes inflicted serious damage on ships anchored there, and two British sailors lost their lives". (Ref 4)

Roof Fall

Sometimes Death descended, like a hawk
Swooping upon unsuspecting prey,
Thousands of feet below in the dark,
As a sudden shift in the clay
Loosed tons of coal onto unprotected backs.

Up above, the living held their breath,
And tried hard not to succumb
To ever-present fears, as news from beneath
Confirmed some men had died, their tomb
A rock-strewn shroud of unforgiving earth.

Much later, a respectful silence reigned
Behind drawn blinds, as bereaved spouses
Mourned, and as their grief spread
By word of mouth, in some other houses
Couples moved closer together in bed.

Oor Francie
Francis Farmer, 1891-1924

We once shared a bed,
Did wee Francie and me,
For with seven sisters dictating
Matters of privacy and priority,
We four lads - big Eck, yours truly,
Young Bob, and Francie - found ourselves
Closeted together in one small room.

Of course, age-wise, compared with
The other two, Eck and me
Were men almost full-grown,
Strapping miners who chased the coal
From early dawn, hundreds of fathom
Down below, heir to practices that paid
Scant attention, then, to personal safety.

We were, in modern parlance,
Role-models ready made for our
Young brothers, and, despite them
Seeing us at our dishevelled worst,
Always dirt-caked and physically tired,
They too, in turn, bowed to family
Expectation, and joined us underground.

But it was above ground
That our Francie really excelled,
Displaying a level of skill and control
With a ball that earned him praise
From footballing peers, and which soon
Attracted the attention of local club scouts
With an eye for talent and potential.

In due course Francie signed forms
For Cowdenbeath FC, then one of the most
Promising senior grade teams in Fife,
Doing very well in the Second Division,
But with realistic aspirations to secure
Promotion to the cherished First Division,
The foremost echelon in Scottish football.

That was indeed the golden period
Of an abruptly truncated career,
For he'd also taken a wife,
Who'd borne him six healthy children,
Of which the youngest, Robert,
Had been delivered only weeks before
Their world was suddenly blown asunder.

Physically very strong, Francie was a brusher
Ready-made, who'd also taken on responsibilities
Of helping out with the shot-firing
Down below, the blasting out of fresh
Cuts of coal for energetic young strippers
To shovel onto constantly-moving conveyors
That fed endless races of hungry tubs.

He had thus to become familiar
With complex procedures - precision hole-boring,
Stemming, safe-handling of explosives,
Detonators and fuses, firedamp testing
Using a safety lamp - and, most vitally,
How to deal with the potential hazards
Arising from the inevitable shot misfire.

For shot-firing was a very skilled,
So very necessary, yet somewhat dangerous
Operation, and one that just could not
Be carried out in haste, no matter what
Production pressures there were to increase
The output of coal being hoisted up
To the surface during any particular shift.

But Francie was not as superhuman
As he often seemed to be, at times,
Upon the soccer stage - a majestic defender,
And famed scorer of penalty goals,
Who had, nevertheless, in a home cup-tie,
Once stunningly equalised proceedings, inadvertently,
By deflecting the ball into his own net.

And so, if even he could err
In play, he could also do so at work,
As he did do, sadly, in the Spring
Of 1924, when he incautiously went
Forward to inspect an undetonated charge,
A misfire, and breached the procedures that
Underpinned safe shot-firing practices underground.

Tragically, that error cost him his life,
And deprived his young and growing family
Of a hard-working loving husband and father,
For that unresponsive seemingly impotent charge
Had suddenly exploded, hurling out a huge
Shard of coal that had struck Francie
Full on the temple, killing him instantly.

News of his death, aged only 33 years,
Reverberated amongst the rest of us like
A shock wave, for as 'the bairn' of
Our household, the youngest of eleven brothers
And sisters, now married themselves with children,
Francie, the richly talented son, and family man,
Was especially loved and respected by all.

And that deep respect also extended throughout
The village community itself, for not only
Were his widow and children engulfed by
A spontaneous wave of sympathy and support
From every quarter, but the Miner's Institute
Donated the beautifully engraved stone that marks
Francie's final resting place in Kinglassie cemetery.

Secure for all time, in hallowed ground
Reserved for our family, whose roots
And many branches spread deep and wide
Through village history, it is a place where,
When the grim reaper decides, there will
Also be space enough for me, yet another
Bed to share, this time made of clay.

[A Eulogy, imagined, by his elder brother, Andrew Farmer, 1874-
1950, the author's grandfather.]

The School Run

The working day in a mining community,
Like Kinglassie, often pre empted the dawn,
As men rose and made ready to muscle
After the elusive coal, venturing into places
Denied natural light, at risk from flooding,
And flushed with contaminated air, whilst above,
Youngsters on the edge of wakefulness snuggled
Deeper into bedclothes for a few moments more,
Reluctant to embrace yet another session at school,
And we, as selected emissaries, were no exception.

Departing from red-roofed Lawrence Park,
Atop Pit Road, at precisely twenty minutes
Past eight o'clock, we left the colliery
Wallowing in its own dayshift generated
Cloud of steam, and our miner fathers
Toiling hard many fathoms down below,
To keep us nourished and well clad,
And very grateful for the scholastic opportunities
We were bussing off to grasp,
Where school grass was deemed much greener.

After a final glance at that hovering pall
Of pithead smoke down the mineral line
At Millar's Corner, the usual lingering thought
That those at work so deep beneath
Had already crawled on hands and knees as far
As we'd been driven, took us onwards
To the Commons brae and then Harestanes Farm,
Before looping down past Auchterderran's Crags
And school towards the juxtaposed incongruity
Of parish church, manse, and very public 'Auld Hoose'.

Then forward into an aptly-named Bowhill,
And upwards, our bus labouring, and briefly
Sandwiched between pithead baths and cooling tanks
Of a multi-shafted Victorian deep bore
For coal, before then breasting the rise
Into Jamphlars, perhaps once – as its name

Suggests – carpeted with flowers, but now
Bedecked only by pond and gorse grown rampant
Around a sundry array of grey slag heaps,
Merging with the grime from near-neighbour Brighills.

Beneath the little hamlet devoted to mining,
Seams beyond the reach of the mightier Bowhill
Were stripped bare, whilst up above them
An enormous steepness, the fabled Eliza Brae,
Seemingly rubbed shoulders with an avenue
Of cloud-fleeced trees that we'd reach only
With difficulty, or occasionally not at all,
If our engine finally expired, albeit appropriately,
Alongside a hedged plantation of engraved stones,
There to await resuscitation, or a tow back home.

And home base was not too far away,
For just beyond the brow of the elongated hill
Lay the little town of Lochgelly, at times
Fenced securely in behind wagons trundling between
The Nellie and the Jenny Gray, sister collieries
Flanking cobbled outreaches of Auchterderran Road,
Where miners lived in Coal Company abodes,
And buses retired for inspection and repair
After Eliza's inclined strain, as we then aboard,
Being abruptly set free, sprinted for our connection.

For we were but halfway to where
We most needed to be, no later than nine,
Which was, by then, only twenty more
Minutes of time, and so without further delay,
We'd clamber into yet another of Alexander's
School line, to then bounce and sway past
The Co-op, the library, and Stahly's best ham,
Towards Lumphinans, where the redoubtable Abe Moffat
Had been raised to spend a lifetime fighting
For miners rights, both above and below ground.

It was the injustices of the Great Lock-Out
Of 1921 that fashioned the industrial
Politics of young firebrand Abe, as union unrest
Within the coalfields now behind us – at Kinglassie,

Bowhill, Lochgelly, and Lumphinans itself – concentrated
Into bruising confrontations between pickets and police
At Cowdenbeath, then the location of a plethora
Of collieries, with men to match, and where
The High Street – our next and final destination
By bus – saw militancy akin to outright war.

Of course, as our overloaded bus sped left
Past the greyhound stadium and into High Street,
We had more mundane objectives in mind
Than those enacted there thirty years before.
For it was vital to scamper the remaining lengthy
Rise of Stenhouse Street, our senses assailed
By a steam-belching No.7 colliery nearby,
And into an imposing but decidedly listing Beath High
In time to beat the dreaded playground roll call,
Or face the prospect of some onerous punishment chore.

The likelihood that Cowdenbeath, and our school
In particular, were sitting upon coal was self-evident,
For the three-storey structure had been sufficiently
Undermined for its ground level suite of rooms
To have become virtually subterranean at on end,
A subsidence constantly reminding pupils that the surfeit
Of colliery sites, and associated surface paraphrenalia,
Visible from top floor windows, not only attested
To the town's impeccable mining pedigree, but also
That men still worked directly beneath their feet.

Perhaps, after years of walking corridors
With a built-in skew, or watching our footballs
Roll only one way in the gym, inevitably,
Despite the uplifting pedagogy underway each day,
Thoughts about future employment would also
Downwards stray, as if unable to resist
The lure of the mine, and in those
Of us travelling in from afar, and back again,
Through communities shaped by generations of commitment
To coal, that pull from the past was stronger still.

At the coalface, Adam Currie,
Bowhill Colliery, early 1950s

Homage to the Bard

I sat by the coal fire, snug in an armchair,
A child maybe, but one who was soon absorbed
Into the atmosphere of an essentially adult occasion.

For the living-room had filled with large men,
Each freshly scrubbed and shaved, and looking ill at ease
In their waist-coated Sabbath best.

Outside, the night air had grown raw enough
To freeze breath, and the first signs of hoar frost
Had begun to glisten on the hedgerows.

For the year had not long since turned,
And it was time, once again, for stalwarts
Of the Burns Club to polish up their favourite songs.

Our house, cosily warm, and with an overstrung piano,
Offered them an opportunity for the uninhibited
Rendering of both verse and music of the bard,

An opportunity they always exploited to the full,
For the very rafters soon resounded to the strains
Of 'Duncan Gray cam here to woo' and the like,

As they rejoiced, albeit temporarily, in the perceptions
Of another, in bawdy refrain or sweet love song,
His music opened the flood-gates of oft-stifled emotions,

The movingly expressed emotions of a real man's man,
Voiced by real men, whose work-roughened exteriors
Concealed an inner sensitivity all too clearly on show.

When the session was finally over, they had some tea,
Holding the fragile bone-china cups in hands
Much better suited to the pickaxes and shovels

That they would all too soon be wielding,
For in just a few hours time, far down below,
They would be stripping out seams of coal.

Mining Memories

We rose very early in the morning,
Even before the dawn had cracked,
Those of us who went mining
For coal. Boots, studded with tacks,
Clomped through cobbled streets, dark
And deserted, as we made our way
To the head of the mine, loathe to work
In a place where night never became day.

No natural light reached down there,
Only light from the lamp on my head,
Held by a strap, and whose beam in air
Made thick by coal dust, was reluctant to spread,
So it hung, suspended in the blackness
Through which it passed, until it struck
Coal, glistening with rivulets of wetness,
Before rebounding back into the dark.

Although there were others toiling near,
It was easy to imagine yourself to be
Alone. In the silences you could hear
The roof creaking, as it tried to free
Itself from the grip of struts, straining to keep
It from raining an avalanche of coal
Upon the back of anyone seeking to strip
Out its black veins of fossil fuel.

When machines were being used,
Cutting deep into the layers of shale,
Rotating blades trying to prise loose
The elusive coal, a veritable gale
Of noise, of gigantic proportion, reverberated
Down the network of rough-hewn
Tunnels, trying very hard to escape,
A cacophony of sound without tune.

Yet, when the long shift was finished,
And I was freed from being down there,
My love of life remained undiminished
As I began to taste sweet fresh air,
And felt sunlight, touching me through the gloom
At the mouth of the mine. Inside, I prayed,
As I left that man-made womb
Of clay, alive, and walked out into day.

Foundations

A sandy-complexioned daughter
Of reformation, her ample frontage
Decorously columnar,
She publicly embraced education
Almost as the century turned.

A repository of learning,
That was what
She was supposed to be,
And surely was,
For so many like me.

And yet, appearances deceived,
For her structured skew,
Her girdered back brace,
Perhaps unfairly, imbued her
With an uncultured face.

It was the coal, of course,
Holes wormed out by drill
Directly beneath,
That distorted the balance
Of 'Old Beath' on the hill.

And so she sat proud,
Amongst mined ash and redd,
A phoenix by day,
In uneven decline,
Bedded into that shifting clay,

Overseeing a playground sprawl
Of prefabrication
And sanitation, as annexed Art
And 'Philosophie Domestica',
Cohabited with Nature's flushed calls.

Inside, the subterranean gloom
Of basement classes,
Mainly a male craft preserve,
Was only lightened by passing flashes
Of navy-knickered thigh,

As up above, two floors high,
Exclamations of 'Eureka',
Or other such scholarly phrases,
Evocatively conveyed
That these were the best days,

Of young lives made richer
By just being there,
For 'SURGO IN LUCEM'
Was, in deed, a legacy,
A sound foundation for life.

Though now excised from the landscape
Like some imperfection,
Her place is assured
In the affections she'd help shape,
Our gratitude endures.

The Fife Coal Company

Background

A Record Book of Long Service

In August, 1945, largely due to the Chairman, Charles Augustus Carlow, the Company produced a book entitled "Record Book of Veteran Employees in the Service of The Fife Coal Company Ltd". It contains a personal photograph and synopsis of the working life and leisure pursuits of each of 242 miners drawn from the many collieries and mining villages across Fife. Criteria for entry is to be at least 65 years of age, to have served 40 years or more with the Company.

The book represents a unique social record of the work patterns and community interests within the mining families of Fife during the first half of the last century. It confirms that the miner did indeed have an active and varied life above ground, incorporating personal interests often energetically useful to the wider community. These veterans, through their strength, endurance and loyalty, despite the hardships imposed by two World Wars, helped keep enough coal flowing out of the pits to meet Britain's increasing demands for it. They were, to a man, a generation to be proud of. (Ref 7)

Authors Note
Andrew Farmer – my grandfather – features in the Book of Veteran Service. It does not for him – nor for any of the others – deal with any domestic matters. He married, raised a family of 8 children, and 4 of his 5 sons became long-serving miners themselves. This on-going pattern of service across several generations within mining families was quite common back then, when King Coal still reigned supreme within the Kingdom of Fife.

SERVICE

RECORD BOOK OF VETERAN EMPLOYEES

FOREWORD

THIS book has been prepared for the purpose of providing an interesting record of those still in our employment who attained the age of sixty-five on or before the 15th August, 1945, and have worked with us for 40 years or more. The Personnel Department have been at great pains to secure accuracy, and it is hoped that they have succeeded in collecting correct information.

In the middle of the book will be found a few facts and anecdotes touching upon events and personalities of a date before 1906, after which any incidents of note may be within the recollection of readers.

To all whose service is recorded in this book I send greetings and good wishes, and my hope is that the other "Old Timers" will find this record as interesting to them as it is to myself.

A. Augustus Carlow

Chairman and Managing Director.

LEVEN,
11th March, 1946.

Published by The Fife Coal Company, individual copies to 242 veteran emplyees

Men Only

At the top of Pit Road they had fashioned
Themselves a communal seat out of a discarded
Railway sleeper. There they would gather
Each working day, clearly addicted to fresh air,

And the need to expunge, through banter and chat,
The almost intolerable tensions of having to work
At the face. Men sharing fears and ribald thoughts
With their mates, but careful to be out of earshot

Of those left behind indoors. The children and wives
Whose continued well-being gave some purpose to lives
Spent stripping out knee-high seams of coal,
In the dark, deep down in a god-forsaken hole.

The Tossing School

The best exponents have practised
Well, and are adept at throwing a pair
of pennies, balanced on a callused hand,
Just high enough up into the air
To ensure their synchronised
Return back down to the ground.

For if they can twist and twirl
In perfect unison, and land flat,
Each with the King's head upwards,
Then the thrower has won, and is able
To pocket any stake money put forward
Into the kitty, which is usually a cloth cap

Provided by one of the assembled crowd
Of miners, gathered at their secret Sunday
Place, to savour a taste of illegality,
And to wager more than any can afford to pay
Upon a toss of coins, and the possibility
That each will proffer its regal face.

Auld Andra

By far the most arresting feature of his rugged face
Was a bristling white moustache, slightly tobacco-stained
In the middle, that always seemed to tickle my chin
When he bent down for a hug. And so I would feign
Mock horror each time the shaggily unshaven countenance
Brushed, like sandpaper, across my own virgin skin.

And when I did this, a bellow of hoarse laughter
Would echo from lungs that seemed to agonize
Over even a normal breath, and then a rasping wheeze
Would rattle deep down in his chest, a recognised
Sign of the bronchial strain that followed soon after
Mild exertion, a clear symptom of advanced lung disease.

For grandad had been a miner, a hewer of coal,
Working more years than he would probably care to say,
Leaving school as a boy of twelve, then to be thrust
Underground, with a tilly lamp to keep darkness at bay,
Spending too many hours in an ill-ventilated hole,
Breathing air not quite free of its insidious dust.

The toil was devilish hard, so back-breakingly arduous,
And danger was a constant visitor to the face,
For trapped pockets of gas could be suddenly set free
During the cutting of new seams, and lethally poisonous
Or explosive fumes would waft into the working space,
A creeping death that no one could see.

Yet, despite the numerous slightly raised weals
Upon his face and limbs, coloured faintly blue
By coal dust getting under skin not quite healed,
And a limp, caused by an untreated foot fracture,
Grandad had been lucky, for he was one of the few
To avoid an injury of a seriously incapacitating nature.

And even though I was then young in years,
I could sense that he derived a great deal of pleasure
In imagining for me, perhaps because I was of the generation
That had inherited a promising post-war world, expectations
For a good life that seemed real enough, then, to reassure
Him that I need never crawl his seams of fear.

Andrew Farmer, who was born on 9th April, 1874, has recently retired, after spending all his working days since he was 12 years of age in coal mining.

Coming to Kinglassie from Hill of Beath when he was a little boy, Andrew commenced his coal mining career at Kirkness Colliery in 1886. Since then, with the exception of three years at Buckhaven, when he was employed at Muiredge Colliery, he worked at Bowhill (6 years), Dunnikier (1 year) and Kinglassie (33 years).

Andrew's one great interest outside mining has been farming, and he has worked on farms in Kinglassie district during most of his leisure hours—a healthy hobby and a serviceable one to his farming friends.

ANDREW FARMER,
35 Burnside Cottages,
KINGLASSIE.
KINGLASSIE COLLIERY.

Andrew Farmer, the author's grandfather.

Extract from 'Record Book of Veteran Employees' of Fife Coal Company. Pub. 1945.

The Bridal Path

The road itself is quite narrow, pot-holed
In places, and neatly bisects more than one farm
As it meanders through the open countryside,

Looking for all the world like a tarmac ribbon
Threaded together with drooping strands of telephone
Wire, hanging, at intervals, from creosoted poles.

Bordered on both sides for most of its length
By fields, with the occasional wood thrown in
For good measure, it has only one footpath,

A shallow covering of compacted bing dross
That keeps encroaching weeds at bay, just wide
Enough to hold two people walking side by side.

During the working day, if viewed from overhead,
The road can be seen for what it is, the only
Stretch of highway between two mining villages,

That seem content to hide beneath their own
Self-generated clouds of dust, smoke and steam,
A surface legacy of the underground rape of virgin seam.

But on the Sabbath, when the huge winding wheels
At each pit-head finally come to rest, that ledge
Of clay begins to assume a life all of its own,

For there are no charabancs running then,
And the few who could afford the luxury of a car,
Have almost certainly gone for a drive elsewhere,

Leaving the way clear for local lads, and lasses,
Who have toiled long and hard every other day,
To venture out of doors for a breath of fresh summer air.

Soon the footpath begins to bear the scuffs and treads
Of at least a hundred strolling feet, and witnesses
The many covert glances of eyes too shy to meet,

For it is there, somewhere along that well-trodden
Track, that secret dreams suddenly take shape,
As two hearts begin to beat at a faster pace,

At the possibility that the future may proffer
More than just the grind of paid domestic chores,
Or the shoring up of roof-props down in the depths below.

As summer fades, and red-gold leaves form upon
The roadside trees, whispered promises are made,
And the seeds of another generation are sown.

Mary, Queen Of Scots, Once Slept Here

The grey waters of the loch,
Caressed by the retreating rays
Of an evening sun, shimmer
With flecks of reflected gold, its surface
Ruffled by a flotilla of rowing boats.

Between the manned little craft, attached
To hand-held lines, cork floats bobbing
Erratically upon a soft swell, create
Their own widening circles of ripple
Which meet, and coalesce into nothingness.

Beneath each float, dancing to every
Nuance of current, there hangs a deception,
A hooked enticement for any hungry
Or unwary inhabitant of these murky depths,
Cunningly dressed up as alluring bait.

For Loch Leven, its wooded island
Appropriately castle-bedecked as befits
A very distinguished historical past,
Is an anglers paradise, its fresh waters
Available, under permit, for fishing.

And so, for many of the menfolk
From nearby villages, like Kinglassie itself,
The chance to fish together in such
Superbly tranquil and beautiful surroundings
Seems far too good to miss,

Particularly for those of mining ilk,
For unlimited open space and clean air
Is the perfect antidote to their dire
Working conditions below ground, a relaxant
To replenish lungs – and larders back home.

"SERVICE"

Alexander Blair, born on 20th January, 1880, came to Bowhill Colliery in 1897 after he had acquired his initial experience in mining at Dunnikier Colliery. Still employed as a packer, he is now in his forty-ninth year at Bowhill.

In his youth Alex. was a well-known boxer and won the Fife Middle Weight Championship at the age of 20. It is very probable that he was inspired to this achievement by the fact that in the previous year he had "stayed the distance" with Bobby Dobbs, the great American Welter Weight boxer. Also a well-known pigeon fancier, he added to his laurels by winning the Pigeon Racing Championship of West Fife in 1945.

ALEXANDER BLAIR,
26 Gammie Place,
Cardenden.

BOWHILL COLLIERY.

Alexander Blair.

Extract from 'Record Book of Veteran Employees' of Fife Coal Company. Pub. 1945.

Phantom of the Rows

It was winter of 1947,
And it had snowed heavily
That year, and I'd acquired
A homemade sledge to share
With my friends, like Mary.

She lay snug beneath me,
Our knees only inches above
Hard-packed snow, as we
Hurtled down the steepness
That was Old Pit Road

And then up a rutted rise
Into twin rows of cottages
Where only mining families lived,
As fathers helped hew out coal
From seams many fathoms below.

Mary's mother was village bred,
And famous, for it was she
Who'd seen, and, indeed, who'd been
Pursued by the dreaded Phantom
Himself, night prowler of the rows.

Hideously disfigured, he shunned
The sun by day, hiding
In abandoned tunnels, down below,
Emerging only in darkness, to lurk
Where no human ought to be.

A fantasy founded in village
Mining lore, and inherited by children,
Like Mary and me, ever more
Willing to believe in what can
Never be, than in safe reality.

All that Glisters. . .

Decades have passed since it was razed
To the ground, the exhausted mine filled in,
And lush grass planted where once houses
Had been, yet I can still remember

Rows of slate-roofed cottages merging
Into a backcloth of ash, a mountain
Of waste hewed out with the coal,
But, like litter, left behind to spread
Dust into every nook and cranny
When an east wind decided to blow.

And beneath the layers of pit-grime,
Faces, too long starved of sunlight,
Had the pallor of permanent tiredness.

Huge winding wheels, straddling the pithead,
Never seemed to stop, nor did the steam engines
Shunting wagons in the yard; surface activities
To match the frenetic rape of virgin
Seams underground, in unlit tunnels flushed
With stale air and almost unbearable sound.
And since every day noises were unable to fill
The silences left behind when the mine stopped
Working, even clocks ticked quieter on a Sunday.

The one day when women, shedding a drabness
Reserved for the rest of the week,
Were proud to be seen in Sabbath best,
Whilst the men, having exchanged their uniform
Coal-dust disguise for a clean face of their own,
No longer looked all the same.

And they seemed content just to sit, and listen,
But not necessarily to believe every pulpit story
Told, for their God, then, was a glistering seam
Of new coal.

End of an Era

Only yesterday, with the long shift finally done,
And bodies and clothes well covered in grime,
We had, as usual, simply staggered back home,
To rid ourselves of the stench from the mine.

A few, perhaps, to wallow in an enamelled bath,
With running water on tap for a wash and scrub,
But most of us, squatting by the fire for warmth,
Had to make do with a pot-filled zinc tub.

But today, we stand naked, sharing a steamy haze,
Showering away our daily layer of coal,
Watching, as rivulets form on the surrounding glaze,
Before vanishing down the nearest drain-hole.

And once outside, we'll feel rather out of place,
A trifle uncomfortable at smelling so clean,
Saddened that the miner with his coal-black face,
Will no longer be a part of the village scene.

Entrants for local 'Coal Queen' competition line up for the judges, in Kinglassie Miners Institute, in the early 1950s. Author's parents are spectating at top right in photo.

The Man who Shot an Albatross

With three generations before him
Hewing out the self-same coal,
Perhaps it was not surprising
That he himself decided
To extend those mining roots
Even more, by also opting
To pursue that fossil ore.

But it was sport that consumed
His prime, and leisure time,
Stroking red leather past fumbling
Slips, or driving an indented
Ball betwixt tee and hole
With practised iron aplomb,
Come hail, rain, or shine.

Even after a long nightshift
Stint below, he and a brace
Of brushers would stop off
At the clubhouse, and against
A backdrop of dawn chorus,
They'd vie for lowest score,
Making birdies, eagles, and occasionally,
Even shooting a rare albatross.

And although he's now passed on,
That Royal and Ancient sporting man,
He's not really gone too far,
For his ashes have been
Laid to rest just where
Old friends are certain to call,
Deep beneath the bunker sand
Of their course's toughest par.

Queen of The Dance

By consensus
Of those present in Miners' Institute
On that special occasion,
The married, the engaged to be,
Or the simply uncommitted
Stepping out for a few drinks,
And a chance to dance
Most of the night away,
It was now about time
To select their newest Coal Queen.

Of course, by tradition,
And on a purely voluntary basis,
Only grown-up daughters,
Or perhaps young wives,
Of genuine colliery toil,
The fair maids spawned by,
Or married to,
Hewers of very local coal,
Were eligible to enter
This singularly prestigious village event.

Importantly too, it was neither
Exploitative nor demeaning,
But was simply great fun,
A post-war expression of social exuberance
To compensate, albeit temporarily,
For the abject harshness
Of just working deep down there,
And focusing upon the public
Veneration of the village's beautiful best
In annual Coal Board competition.

And so when the dancing pairs
In close embrace, finally relinquished floor space
To the grand parade, ladies involved made
Hasty repair to both face and hair,
And discreet adjustments to dresses
Designed to flare attractively just below
Nyloned knees, their facial expressions ranging
From coy nervousness to a confidence
Inspired by past success, and yet, each still
Exuding a beauty much deeper than mere skin.

As their musically-backed perambulations
Around the hall drew deserved applause
For a teasingly pleasing display of elegance
Fit to grace any court of King Coal,
It was easy to transpose time and place,
And to imagine their matriarchal forbears,
Perhaps sturdier of frame and limb, and clad
In apparel decidedly more threadbare,
Clambering from a deep hole in the ground
Bearing a heavy load of coal ore.

Between A Rock and A Hard Place

It sat beside the fire,
A coal fire, back then,
Upholstered, cushioned, and square,
As just one of a pair
Of ordinary armchairs,
And yet, more than that,
For it was his chair,
And even when he wasn't around,
Was quite out of bounds
To visitors, including church ministers,
And certainly to youngsters too,
Be they niece or nephew,
Or a son - like me.

Of course, late 1940's,
Just immediately post-war,
Family life in working-class homes
Was particularly harsh and austere,
By courtesy of food rationing,
Low wages, and an economy
Still suffering from battle fatigue.

And there was no TV,
Not then, to distract
From the inherent drudgery
Of everyday domestic routine;
Only the wireless,
That stolid knob-faced
Consumer of bottled electricity,
Could extend an ear
To a world of erudition,
Entertainment, and newsworthy events
Almost beyond comprehension;
It was indeed a magic box
Of whines, crackles, and clicks.

But the live performances
Were reserved for Saturday evenings
Once his working week was over,
And the football results, and pools
Had been meticulously checked
Before debate, over a pint or two,
With mates at the village pub;
For then, it was take-away time,

With shop-fried fish and chips,
Duly vinegared and paper-wrapped,
Being rushed home for our consumption,
Whilst we listened to and laughed at
His tall tales from that chair.

That was the best time
For us to gather together
As a family, in a week
Largely dominated by, for him,
Long shifts at the local colliery;
At least, for that brief spell
There were chips, and chuckles, to share.

A togetherness short-lived however,
For morning saw Sunday dawn,
And with it came, for him,
The customary long lie in bed,
With newspapers and cigarettes to hand,
A chance to rest his over-taxed
Frame for a few precious hours,
Before the next six days of graft
Down below, cutting the coal seams
That kept us in food and clothes,
And enabled a schoolboy like me
To secure for myself a future
Free from the tyranny of the mine.

A freedom for all,
As it duly came to pass,
Alas, a few decades further on,
When those fossilised bands of ore
Glistened no more, and pit closures
Rocked an industry to its core;
And for lifelong hewers of coalface, like him,
Redundancy was terminal, the final hard place.

Pit Closure

Although it is long past dawn, the morning
Air is cold enough to transform our breath
Into pockets of visible condensation, forming
A puff of instant cloud around each mouth
That has something to say, or shout about,
Within the large crowd gathered around
The pithead gates, or which is simply breathing out
Like mine, not quite ready to make sound.

From our makeshift platform I can see him,
Bent, huddling close to a pillar to avoid the cold,
Not looking in my direction, his profile grim
And unyielding, my dad, a miner of old,
Who used to be strong enough to break a nail
With powerful hands, who could work all day,
And then some more, who now looks so frail,
So very old, and who should have stayed away.

The proposed closure of this pit isn't his fight,
He with his memories, thoughts of the hard times,
When he got injured, and how only the sight
Of his sickly, underfed children spurred him
To hold on, to beat the cold and the chilling damp
Of a new mine, the muscle-sapping task
Of tunnelling through the dark, with a tilly lamp
To both light the way and ignite pockets of gas.

This mine is on its last legs, having exhausted
Its coal, it is uneconomic, it will require
More money to keep it open than it will cost
In redundancy payments to those who can retire
Early from the backbreaking unhealthy toil
Of digging for fresh coal, deep underground
Where daylight cannot reach, where dust soils
Even the air that is circulated around.

And so I stand up and make my speech,
Suggesting that the mine should not be spared,
Using emotive phrases calculated to reach
Deep into the pockets of men who now care
More for themselves than they do for the past,
Who have now given much, in body and soul,
To work a mine whose coal cannot last,
And to whom redundancy is an acceptable goal.

As expected, the vote has gone my way,
Yet, I'm depressed, and feeling rather sad,
Wilting under the pressures of a trying day,
And wanting so much to make up with my dad,
Huddled down there, looking so old and ill,
Pointedly ignoring me as he turns to go,
Obviously disappointed in my role at the kill,
Reluctant to accept his old pit has to close.

Twa Auld Foggies

They'd usually preferred the nightshift
Stint, when darkness above almost matched
The absolute blackness down below,
Where they'd relished the task of blasting
And brushing roadways into compliance,
Meeting the demands of dayshift strippers
Intent upon removing yet another seam
Of coal, both speedily and safely,
Whilst they themselves went home to bed.

But not immediately of course,
For the bonus of such night work
Was to be able to savour
The awakening of a brand new day,
To enjoy the contagious chirpiness
Of the dawn chorus, and to breathe
Morning air that invigorated sufficiently
For even a pre-breakfast nine holes
To be contemplated, before succumbing,
Finally, to a snatch of daytime sleep.

For these were, then, halcyon years
Immediate post-war, when the promise
Of communal prosperity and job security
Seemed firm as fresh-hewn coal;
But, alas, that was not to be,
For the spectre of mass redundancy
Soon stalked seams unexpectedly bereft
Of black gold, thus inviting 'the dole',
That old scourge of miners' rows,
To begin haunting there once more.

But between that distant yesteryear
And today, there had to be
Other jobs, less exacting and decidedly
Less vital than mining had ever been,
For they'd family responsibilities to meet,

With dependents to be fed and clad,
And, latterly, elderly or ill relatives
To care for, commitments that fully absorbed
Both time and mind, and which scuppered,
For them, any realistic prospect of self-fulfilment.

Of course, as first cousins, they were,
Indubitably, the last generation in a long line
Of coal hewers to be thus employed,
And now, mature octogenarians both,
Who've outlived their peers by years,
They depend upon each other for company,
A family legacy to share with pride,
Particularly over a fresh-brewed mug of tea,
And convivial exchanges of nostalgic reflections
That keep daily problems in proper perspective.

Note: The maternal half of the author's family have been steeped in the coal industry for at least four generations. Two of them, his Uncle Sandy (Alex Mathieson), and his uncle's first cousin, Davie (David Gillan), are still surviving. At 82 years and 84 years respectively, they are now the eldest men in their village (Dundonald, in Fife). This poem is an affectionate tribute to them

THOMAS ERSKINE,
29 Croall Street,
KELTY.

LINDSAY COLLIERY.

Like his veteran brother, Peter, of Cowdenbeath No. 7 Colliery, **Thomas Erskine,** born in 1876, commenced his mining career with the Callendar Coal Company at the age of 11. In 1894 he followed his brother's example and entered the employment of the Company at Lindsay Colliery, with this distinction that he has remained at the Lindsay throughout the whole of his 51 years' service with the Company. Experienced in all types of underground work, Tom was only obliged to relinquish underground duties in 1939.

To mention the name of Erskine in Kelty is to mention the word bagpipes—they are synonymous. Tom spent 50 happy years with Kelty Pipe Band, and in 1914-1918 served as a piper in the Argyll and Sutherland Highlanders.

Thomas Erskine.

Extract from 'Record Book of Veteran Employees' of Fife Coal Company. Pub. 1945.

End Of The Line

There she stands, a smouldering giant,
With her steam billowing in the rime
Of a cold dawn. So proud and defiant
To the end, this colossus of the line.

Hot air currents shimmer and rise
Above an iron shell within which burns
A fresh charge of coal. With a slow hiss,
An injection of steam, the huge wheels turn.

Her progress is lumbering and very slow,
As amidst belching smoke and escaping steam
She begins her final journey. The fiery glow
Of her firebox adding warmth to a wintry scene.

This clanking denizen of raw steam power
Puffs, pulling her last load this January
Morning. With the mine not working anymore,
Tomorrow, she will be just a memory.

A Green and Pleasant Land Again

The valley, strangely silent, was once full of sound
When the mine was working, as half-naked men drilled,
And hewed, and shovelled, and died, deep underground.
Toiling too hard perhaps, to ensure tubs were filled
With coal, the lifeblood of a close-knit community
Which had grown, and thrived, far above hard-won seams,
That, in the end, had been unable to provide immunity
Against a redundancy so endemic of the colliery scene.
And now, along with the coal, redd bings, and grime,
A uniquely hard way of earning a living has gone.
Where once there were the surface paraphernalia of a mine,
There are trees, and grassed fields that cows graze upon,
A land temporarily possessed, now exorcised of demon ore
Below, has returned to how it was half a century before.

Going Back

First impressions deceived. The survival of ancient structures,
Blythe's Tower, the hump bridge, and the Mitchell Hall,
Were distractions. There were fundamental changes elsewhere

The familiar trappings of the old pithead itself
Had long since gone, excised from the rural landscape
Like some erstwhile carbuncle from unblemished skin,

And the miners' rows that had huddled, albeit uncomfortably,
Under the giant shadows cast by a constantly growing bing
Of ash, dross and shale, had also been totally razed.

Now, only a few of the original cottages remain in Burnside,
Their unkempt gardens and flaking window frames
contrast sharply
With the extensive and somewhat elaborate renovations next door.

And yet, despite these cosmetic labours to remove half a century
Of accumulated coal dust and grime, just a few steps beyond
Each garden gate, as ever, the ageless Lochty still flows,

A winding thread of water, no doubt retaining its fair share
Of sewage and resident rats, but no longer required to segregate
From the village, those who crawled seams deep down below.

Instead, housed upon its pithead shore, is a quasi-suburban
Influx of commuter abodes, double-glazed, and with patio doors,
A contemporary antithesis of what had been there all these years
before,

The street that was once home, smoothly resurfaced with a mix
Of molten pitch wedded to hard-core, now seems so quiet and still,
Almost as if children did not live or play there anymore.

The Lady's Not for Spurning

Slow grown,
And deep bedded
In a womb of clay,
She'd lain there for aeons
And a day,
Until the men came,
To shaft her,
And to rip her innards away.

Though her airways
Clogged with dust,
And her guts
Exploded, belching hot fire,
Still they persisted,
Toiling with rapacious haste
To strip her bare,
Violating her virginal core.

A hysterectomy
Performed without anaesthetic,
Coal cut out at pace,
Leaving her bereft
Of anything useful inside,
An abandoned shell
Completely denuded of pride,
Ashamed of her landscaped face.

And like so many more
Simply put to pasture,
Their wombs now tombs
To imprudent coalmining lore,
She watched, as her pillaged ore
Burned holes in an ozone sky,
Grateful that Mother Nature
Had fashioned herself a fitting reply.

Shadows in The Dark

Looking back, there was something incredibly secretive
About the pit, a workplace shrouded in mystery,
Where only grown-ups ever went, particularly the men,
And which seemed to make them tired, so depleted
Of energy when they returned at the end of the day,
To recuperate, before leaving to begin all over again..

It was what the old, apparently, had once done,
And which they frequently reflected upon, at length,
As if addicted to the retelling of experiences, so trying,
So debilitating, that their effects still lingered on,
In faces etched by strain, and bodies robbed of strength,
Yet holding on, like shadows in light that is dying.

Survivors

Those half-remembered fragmented experiences,
Of war, food rationing, the wax
And wane of coal, can weave together,
Through chat, into a tapestry of substance,
Of significance to the lives touched,
Or shaped, by the hardships inherent
In difficult times, shared by so many.

A harsh collective nostalgia made poignant
By their survival, and by reminiscences
That embraced absent friends, and forbears,
Who'd helped paint that final canvas
Of reflections, yet one tempered by regrets
That their hopes for a better future
Were to remain largely unrealised.

Of course, there had been a camaraderie
Around then, which welded individual resolves
Into a spirited communal stoicism
Well able to withstand the iniquities
Of a system of class and privilege
That they'd simply inherited, and which,
They too, had pledged themselves to change.

Although, perhaps with a few misgivings,
At least in part, for as youngsters,
Sleeping close together in alcoves too small,
Or wearing garments visibly threadbare
And oft used before, they somehow knew
That their well-being was founded upon things
Money couldn't buy – like friendship, and love.

But now, alas, social change has disrupted
The closeness of both family and community ties,
And so, unlike that mutually supportive ethos
Of Yesterday, when problems were often shared,
And solved, across different generations,
Almost akin to recurring scenarios in time,
Today, human tribulations are shouldered alone.

The author, Andrew Farmer, with grandson, Cai Farmer, August 2004.

Insert: Cai's father, Richard, (deceased), crash victim, May 2002.

Like Father, Like Son

My son,
You were the family face,
A true composite of forbears,
Of familiars, like me,
Or granddad, and others
You were too young to know.

Features and characteristics
Defined as of old,
In profile, or smile,
Or colour and boldness of eye,
Reflecting past generations long gone,
And lives left largely untold.

Yet, old genes were reborn
As if new,
Transcending our mere mortality
And time flown,
To be recast in a uniqueness
That was you.

And now, despite your tragic
Very premature demise,
That heredity has not died,
For within that gorgeous little son
Of your own, within Cai,
An essence of family lives on.

Note: Published by the author in his commemorative book, 'Richard and his Greyhounds' (2003), as a family tribute to late son, Richard, who died in May 2002. He is survived by a son, Cai, now 5 years of age.

Last Write

When I die,
Let's call it 'passing away',
    By all means,
Do have a good cry,
But speak no sombre words,
Before granting me the rites
    Of ancient alchemy.

First,
Consume me with fire,
    Burn me dry,
For only then
Can my spirit soar free,
To where birds fly high
    And storm clouds shed tears.

Then,
Bury my ashes deep,
    Embraced by rich fertile earth
Beneath some well-watered tree
Rooted in a special place,
And there to sleep,
To await the birth
    Of new Spring leaves.

And when the sap is rising,
To then bask with them,
    Enjoying the langorous warmth
Of summer sun,
Until, the slow golden flush
Of late Autumn
    Heralds our inevitable downfall.

It would please me
To be recycled just so,
    To take a posthumous trip
Around Mother Nature's garden,
And with my genes
Already in circulation elsewhere,
I'd have become, at last,
A real 'lad o' pairts',
    An essence in constant flow.

Acknowledgements

I could not have produced this book without the specific help and advice of other people. In alphabetical order, I'd therefore like to thank:

George Archibald, Scottish Mining Museum
Roger Cullingham, Thameslink Ltd
Allan Ferrier, friend, of Doonfoot, Ayr
Dan Imrie, ex-miner, fellow writer, Kinglassie
Neil Miller, Archivist, Register House, Edinburgh
Catherine Pryde, Local History Dept, Dunferline Library
Karen Theobald, www.thefurrymonkey.co.uk

Since the loss of our youngest son, Richard, in May 2002, family life can never be the same again.

Without the support of other people, which I gratefully acknowledged in my commemorative book "Richard and his Greyhounds" (2003), we could not have coped.

Of course Richard has left us a grandson, Cai, now 5 years, whom we adore. In time, as he matures, we'll encourage him to learn about and understand the origins of his paternal roots. This book may just be a useful addition to that pool of knowledge. The penultimate poem "Like Father, Like Son" is for Cai, the man. May he grow to respect his paternal grandfather as much as I do mine.

And finally, but not least, I'm grateful, as always, for the patience, support and love of my wife, Freda. She stoically shares and shoulders all.